VISION BOARD
Clip Art Book
Images, Words & Quotes

Vision Borad Clip Art Book

Your FREE Gifts

As a way of saying *Thank You* for your purchase,

I'm offering you tons of goodies.

Scan me

Inside you will discover:

☑ 5 Essential Steps to take *before* creating your vision board.
$9.97 value

☑ Unlock Your Dream Life: 7 Reflection Questions You Must Ask Yourself **$14.97 value**

☑ The Ultimate Planning Tool: 12-Month Goal Intention Cards **$24.97 value**

☑ Digital Vision Board Templates: Now you can carry your inspiration with you anytime, anywhere. **$19.97 value**

☑ 25 Additional Affirmation cards and Quotes **$14.97 value**

☑ 7 Simple Tips for Hosting a Mind-Blowing Vision Board Party! **Priceless**

$85 Value   FREE

Scan the QR Code if you're ready to design your dream life today

Table of Contents

Introduction

Welcome to the 2025 Vision Board Clip Art Book: Powerful Images, Words, and Quotes.

This book is thoughtfully designed to inspire, motivate, and guide you in shaping a vision board that aligns with your goals, values, and dreams for the future. By combining impactful images, inspiring words, and uplifting quotes, you'll have all the tools you need to create a personalized vision board that expresses your aspirations.

PURPOSE OF THE BOOK

The purpose of this vision board clip art book is to simplify the process of creating an effective vision board. This book serves as a one-stop resource as we have provided an extensive selection of powerful images, motivational words, and encouraging quotes. You can dive in and start building a board that represents your unique goals without searching through endless magazines or online images. Vision boards have been shown to help people clarify their desires, stay focused, and manifest their dreams. You will be able to design a board that is both visually appealing and deeply meaningful to you with this book.

THE BENEFITS OF VISION BOARD

1. Clarity of Goals and Desires: A vision board allows you to specify your goals and ambitions. You can define what you truly want to achieve, by selecting images and words that resonate with you.

2. Daily Motivation and Inspiration: The visual representation of your goals keeps you focused and motivated.

3. Improved Visualization and Manifestation: Visualization is a powerful tool, and a vision board brings it to life. If you see your board on a daily basis, your mind will be able to recognize opportunities aligned with your goals, helping you to manifest them.

4. Encourages Positive Mindset and Focus: Vision boards serve as a positive reinforcement of your goals, counteracting negativity and distractions.

5. Tracks Progress and Growth: As you accomplish goals, you'll see how far you've come and be encouraged to set new aspirations, making it a valuable tool for ongoing self-development.

How to Create

MATERIALS REQUIRED

1. A Blank Canvas (e.g poster board, cork board or foam board)

2. Scissors for cutting images, affirmations, quotes etc

3. Glue or adhesive tape for attaching cutouts to the board

4. Markers or color pencils for adding personal touches

STEP-BY-STEP INSTRUCTIONS

Creating a vision board with this clip art book is an enjoyable and inspiring experience! Here's a step-by-step guide to designing a vision board that brings your dreams to life:

Step 1: Set Your Intentions: Start by defining what you truly want in key areas like wellness, family, career, finances, and personal joy. Think deeply about your aspirations and get specific with your intentions.

Step 2: Explore the Clip Art Book: Flip through this book to find images, quotes, and words that spark excitement and represent your goals. Don't be afraid to choose pieces that challenge or surprise you they can lead to growth!

Step 3: Gather Your Supplies: Grab a sturdy surface like a corkboard, poster, or foam board, along with glue, pins, scissors, and any extra decorations you'd like to add, such as stickers or glitter.

Step 4: Experiment with Layout: Place the cut-out images and words on your board and play around with the arrangement. Let your intuition guide you; there's no wrong way to display what resonates with you most.

Step 5: Secure the Pieces: Once you're satisfied with your layout, begin attaching each piece to your board. Use glue for permanence, or opt for pins if you want flexibility to update or shift things over time.

Step 6: Display in a Prominent Spot: Position your vision board in a place where you'll see it often—by your bedside, at your workspace, or in a meditation corner. This will keep you connected to your goals daily.

Step 7: Reflect and Update Regularly: Spend time each day or week reflecting on the images and words on your board. As you achieve milestones or set new goals, refresh your board to reflect your evolving path.

Start Now!

Be Bold

You can have
Results or Excuses
Not Both

Financial freedom

Dream BIG

COMMITTED

RISE AND SHINE

I CAN & I WILL

AIM HIGH

CONNECT

TAKE CHANCES

MAKE A DIFFERENCE

SMILE

LEARN MORE

WORRY LESS

BE CREATIVE

BUILD FAITH

BELIEVE

BE AWESOME

BE COURAGEOUS

WORK HARD

HONEST

WISDOM

BE A LEADER

BRILLIANT

OPTIMISTIC

YOUR BODY CAN STAND ALMOST ANYTHING. IT'S YOUR MIND YOU HAVE TO CONVINCE.

EACH DAY YOU MUST CHOOSE PAIN OF DISCIPLINE OR PAIN OF REGRET

Get fit!

No Excuses

Keep Going

I AM OPEN
to receiving endless abundance

I ATTRACT
opportunities for financial growth

I AM GRATEFUL
for my strong and healthy body

I GET
more fit and healthy everyday

I ENJOY
working out and I love the energy it gives to me

I DON'T STOP
when I am tired, I stop when I am done

I RELEASE
any fear or doubt that stands in the way of my success

I HAVE INFINITE
potential and can do anything I put my mind to

Practice Gratitude and appreciate little thing in life.

Make Your DREAMS HAPPEN

I reward myself regularly for attaining my goals.

"knowing yourself is the beginning of all Wisdom"

FIND JOY IN THE

LITTLE THINGS

live your dream.

BE THE
CHANGE

TAKE
ACTION

NEW MONDAY
NEW WEEK
NEW GOAL

Do
WHAT
you
love

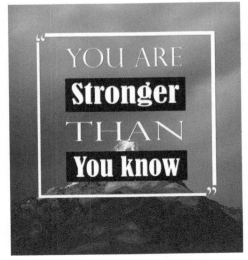

"YOU ARE
Stronger
THAN
You know"

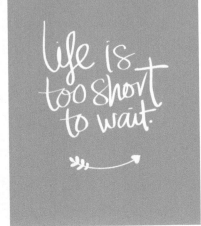

life is
too short
to wait.

BE HAPPY

I AM CAPABLE OF
CREATING A LIFE
FILLED WITH JOY
AND PURPOSE.

I AM OPEN TO
GROWTH AND SEE
EVERY EXPERIENCE
AS A LESSON.

I AM AT PEACE WITH
MY PAST AND
FOCUSED ON
BUILDING MY FUTURE.

MY ACTIONS ALIGN
WITH MY HIGHEST
VALUES AND
INTENTIONS.

I AM WORTHY OF
LOVE AND
RESPECT.

I AM CENTERED AND
CALM IN ALL
SITUATIONS.

MY HEART RADIATES
COMPASSION FOR
MYSELF AND
OTHERS.

I AM DESERVING OF
HAPPINESS AND
WELCOME IT INTO
MY LIFE.

I AM GROWING
AND LEARNING
EVERY DAY.

MY WORDS HOLD
POWER, AND I
CHOOSE THEM
WISELY.

MY LIFE IS FILLED
WITH PURPOSE, AND
I CREATE MEANING
DAILY.

MY BODY IS
HEALTHY, MY MIND
IS CLEAR, AND MY
SOUL IS AT EASE.

A mistake is an opportunity to learn not a reason to give up.

NEW MINDSET → NEW RESULTS

Happiness

Goals

BE UNIQUE

ONE SMALL POSITIVE THOUGHT IN THE MORNING CAN CHANGE YOUR WHOLE DAY

MOVING FORWARD

GOOD VIBES

DREAMS DO NOT WORK UNLESS YOU DO

THERE IS NO DAY WITHOUT GYM

I ATTRACT STRENGTH ENDURANCE & RESILIENCE WITH EVERY WORKOUT I COMPLETE

I AM SO HAPPY & GRATEFUL FOR THE LIFE I HAVE

MY MIND IS CLEAR & FOCUSED

I DESERVE THE BEST AND I ACCEPT ONLY THE BEST

I ATTRACT ABUNDANCE & PROSPERITY INTO MY LIFE

I OVERCOME FEARS BY FOLLOWING MY DREAMS

NEVER GIVE UP STAY STRONG

EVERY DAY I GET CLOSER TO MY DREAMS & GOALS

I AM CONFIDENT IN EXPRESSING MY FEELINGS AND NEEDS IN MY RELATIONSHIPS

I HAVE THE POWER TO CREATE THE LIFE I WANT

Faith

ACCEPT

Meditation

Your sacred space is where you can find yourself again and again

Relax

DO IT NOW!
SOMETIMES
LATER
BECAME
NEVER

Believe

BLESSED!

Keep Calm

STAY FOCUSED

Strength SPIRIT

*be kind

STAY Positive

BE Humble!

GRATEFUL Enjoy

Responsible

GOOD LUCK

Never get so busy making a living that you forget to make a life

"We are most alive when we're in love."

John Updike

LOVE OF MY LIFE

MY heart is YOURS

Love doesn't need to be perfect. It just has to be true

YOU
»–AND–→
ME

Happily Married

Dream WEDDING

We are getting **married**

FAMILY *is* **FOREVER**

"Family means no one gets left behind or forgotten."

David Ogden Stiers

The love of a family is life's greatest blessing

Family Time **is Priceless**

Making Memories

"Count your age by friends, not years. Count your life by smiles, not tears." John Lennon

A faithful FRIEND LOVES to the End

"A friend is someone who knows all about you and still loves you."

Elbert Hubbard

"Hard work beats talent when talent doesn't work hard."
Tim Notke

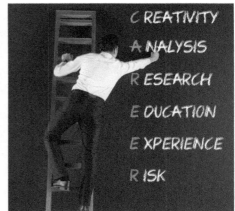

CREATIVITY
ANALYSIS
RESEARCH
EDUCATION
EXPERIENCE
RISK

"The only way to achieve the impossible is to believe it is possible." – Charles Kingsleigh

Dedication

Leadership

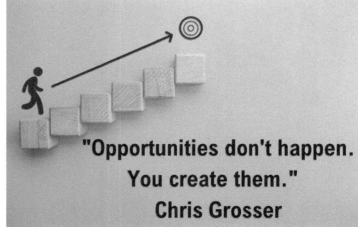

"Opportunities don't happen. You create them."
Chris Grosser

I AM RESILIENT
BECAUSE I LEARN FROM MY CHALLENGES

I AM STRONG
BECAUSE I TRUST IN MY INNER STRENGTH

I AM PEACEFUL
BECAUSE I EMBRACE CALM IN EVERY SITUATION

I AM GROWING
BECAUSE I WELCOME CHANGE AND NEW OPPORTUNITIES

I AM PATIENT
BECAUSE I TRUST IN THE TIMING OF MY LIFE

I AM HOPEFUL
BECAUSE I KNOW GOOD THINGS ARE ON THE WAY

I AM GRATEFUL

I AM STRONG

I AM KIND

I AM CREATIVE

I AM BRAVE

I AM HOPEFUL

Home Sweet Home

Home is not a place it is *a feeling*

welcome ♡HOME♡

Dream Home

I am a loving pet owner

My home is complete with a pet

LEARN AS YOU GROW

KEEP LEARNING

TRAIN -YOUR- mind

TODAY A READER TOMORROW A LEADER

LEARNING NEVER ENDS

Read More

Progress

MASTER'S
Desgree

"The beautiful thing about learning is that no one can take it away from you." – B.B. King

We travel not to escape life
but for life not to escape us

Catch flights, not feelings

"COURAGE IS RESISTANCE TO FEAR, MASTERY OF FEAR, NOT ABSENCE OF FEAR." MARK TWAIN

TIRED FEET HAPPY HEART

We travel because distance and difference are the secret tonic of creativity.

TRAVEL AS MUCH AS YOU CAN, AS FAR AS YOU CAN, AND AS LONG AS YOU CAN. LIFE IS NOT MEANT TO BE LIVED IN ONE PLACE.

Paris

London

Venice

Madrid

Santorini

Florence

Sydney

Dubai

Cairo

Istanbul

Prague

Bangkok

VISION BOARD

This is my year to glow up and shine

Welcome 2025

the year of transformation

2025 is my year to spark joy and inspire!

Ready to shine in 2025

DREAM + WORK = SUCCESS

SLAY

HAPPY NEW YEAR

FEARLESS

BOLD
Brave
Strong

BE
Fearless

Embrace
YOUR
Peace

things
CHANGE
AROUND
you

SHINE
LIKE
→THE→
stars

Focus
on the
GOOD

Never
STOP
learning!

YOU'RE
THE
GREATEST

Wake Up
AND
Smile

KEEP
Calm

There ARE
NO REGRETS

it's a
BEAUTIFUL DAY
to learn

YOU WILL
NEVER HAVE
this DAY
AGAIN

BEAUTIFUL
destina
tions

Things
TAKE
Time

CE LE BRA TION

· TIME ·

You are resilient

CHOOSE HAPPY

STOP
THINGKING
START
DOING

the time -is- now

LIVE SIMPLY LOVE FULLY

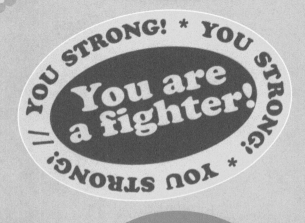

Mental Health Matters

I was kind to myself TODAY

END THE STIGMA

YOU STRONG! * YOU STRONG! // YOU STRONG! * YOU STRONG! //

You are a fighter!

COOL COOL

READY TO WIN

spread love

L♥VE Yourself

Daily dose of happiness

LIFES GOES ON

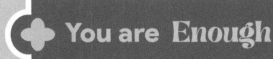

You are Enough

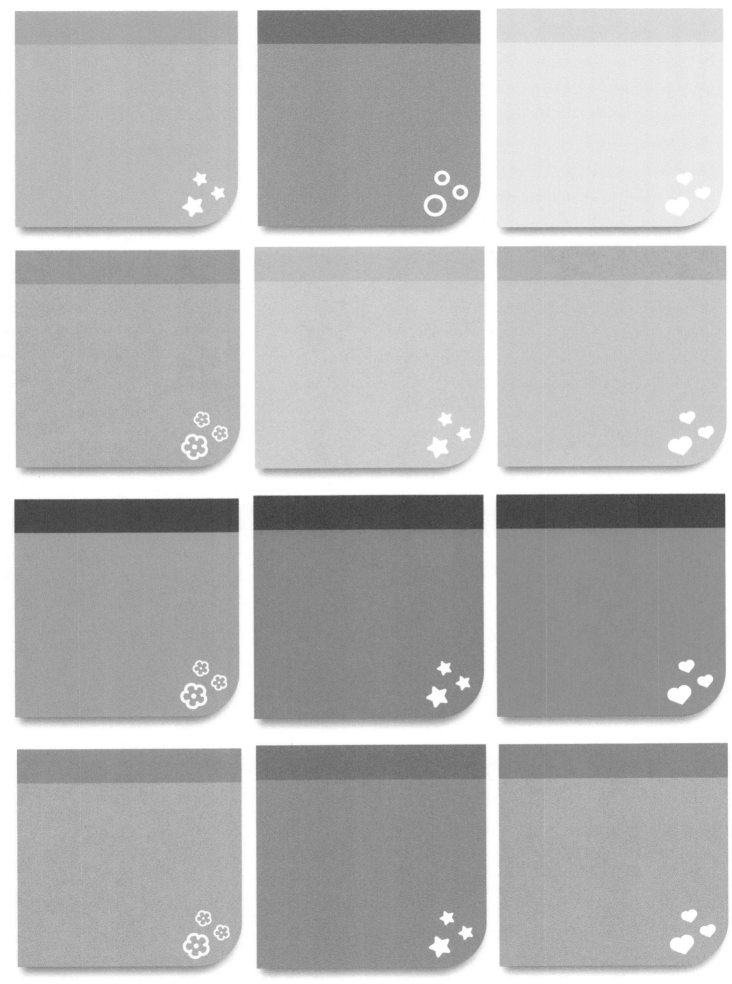

AAAABBBBBCCCC

DDDDEEEEFFFF

GGGGHHHHIIII

JJJJKKKKLLLL

MMMMNNNNOOOO

PPPPQQQQRRRR

SSSSTTTTUUUU

VVVVWWWWWXX

XXYYYYZZZZ

1 1 1 1 2 2 2 2 2 3 3 3 3 3

4 4 4 4 4 5 5 5 5 5 6 6 6 6

7 7 7 7 7 8 8 8 8 9 9 9 9 9

0 0 0 0 0 @ @ @ @ # # # #

* * * * ! ! ! ! (((((

))))) < < < < > > > >

+ + + + + = = = = ? ? ? ? ?

& & & & % % % % $ $

$ $ $ { { } } [[ ]]

"Every positive choice you make plants seeds for tomorrow's success."

Made in the USA
Las Vegas, NV
29 December 2024